© D. C. Thomson & Co. Ltd., 1983.
ISBN 0 85116 290 8

The
Fireside Book

*A picture and a poem
for every mood
chosen by*

David Hope

Printed and Published by
D.C. THOMSON & CO., LTD.
185 Fleet Street, LONDON EC4A 2HS

THE CUCKOO

HIS voice runs before me; I follow, it flies;
   It is now in the meadow and now in the skies;
So blithesome, so lightsome; now distant, now here;
And when he calls " Cuckoo!" the summer is near.

He calls back the roses, red roses, that went
At the first blast of winter, so red and forespent,
With the dew in their bosoms, young roses and dear;
And when he calls " Cuckoo!" the summer is near.

I would twine him a gold cage, but what would he do
For his world of the emerald, his bath in the blue?
And his wee feathered comrades to make him good cheer?
And when he calls " Cuckoo!" the summer is near.

Now, blackbird, give over your harping of gold!
Brown thrush and green linnet, your music withhold!
The flutes of the forest are silver and clear,
But when he calls " Cuckoo!" the summer is here.

Katharine Tynan Hinkson

TIME FOR PLAY

SHE gets up at seven
  And rushes downstairs
  Expecting a day full of fun.
Grandad and she
Make some soldiers of toast,
  Her play has already begun.

After her breakfast
She wants to play " shops ",
  So Grandad must wait to get shaved.
He sets up his market
While she finds her purse
  And counts all the money she's saved.

Later that morning
Her Grandma needs help
  To bake some new biscuits for tea.
She puts on her apron
And rolls up her sleeves:
  What shape are the biscuits to be?

Dinner is over,
So off to the park
   To swing and to see-saw and slide.
Back in the garden
It's out with the pram
   To take her two dolls for a ride.

Hide and seek follows,
Then throwing a ball,
   And making a home in the shed.
Some quick games of Snap
Between tea and a bath,
   Then after a story it's BED!

Marion Elliott

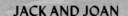

JACK AND JOAN

JACK and Joan they think no ill,
　But loving live, and merry still:
Do their week-day's work, and pray
Devoutly on the holy day.
Skip and trip it on the green,
And help to choose the Summer Queen;
Lash out at a country feast
Their silver penny with the best.

Well can they judge of nappy ale,
And tell at large a winter tale;
Climb up to the apple loft,
And turn the crabs till they be soft.
Tib is all the father's joy,
And little Tom the mother's boy.
And all their pleasure is content;
And care, to pay their yearly rent.

Joan can call by name her cows,
And deck her windows with green boughs;
She can wreaths and tutties make,
And trim with plums a bridal cake.
Jack knows what brings gain and loss;
And his long flail can stoutly toss:
Makes the hedge, which others break;
And ever thinks what he doth speak.

Now, you courtly dames and knights,
That study only strange delights,
Though you scorn the homespun gray,
And revel in your rich array,
Though your tongues dissemble deep,
And can your heads from danger keep,
Yet, for all your pomp and train,
Securer lives the silly swain.

Thomas Campion

SHE WALKS IN BEAUTY

SHE walks in beauty, like the night
    Of cloudless climes and starry skies;
And all that's best of dark and bright
    Meet in her aspect and her eyes:
Thus mellow'd to that tender light
    Which heaven to gaudy day denies.

One shade the more, one ray the less,
    Had half impair'd the nameless grace
Which waves in every raven tress,
    Or softly lightens o'er her face;
Where thoughts serenely sweet express
    How pure, how dear their dwelling-place.

And on that cheek, and o'er that brow,
    So soft, so calm, yet eloquent,
The smiles that win, the tints that glow,
    But tell of days in goodness spent,
A mind at peace with all below,
    A heart whose love is innocent!

Lord Byron

LONDON IN SPRING

THE rain has washed my London clean,
    The wind has swept the dust away,
The rain has made her fresh and green,
    The sun has made her gay!

How prettily she wears her gown
    Of lilac bloom, or blushing rose . . .
How lovely looks my London Town
    Where lush laburnum blows!

Her messengers are on the wing,
    For, somewhere in an apple tree,
A blackbird's singing to the Spring
    His boyish song of glee!

And oh, my heart takes up his lay
    Of rapture felt, and yet unseen—
So lovely London is, so gay,
    So fresh, and cool, and green.

Cassandra Page-Turner

THE OLD LADIES

THEY walked in straitened ways,
  They had not great possessions;
They lived before the days
  When ladies learned professions.

And one was rather mad
  And all were rather trying,
So little life they had,
  So long they spent a-dying.

In spotless white lace caps,
  Just sitting, sitting, sitting,
Their hands upon their laps
  Or occupied with knitting.

And now they all are gone,
  Miss Alice and Miss Ella,
Miss Jane (at ninety-one)
  And poor Miss Arabella.

It seemed as though their lives
  Were wasted more than others':
They would have made good wives,
  They might have made good mothers.

Yet this was their reward:
  Through ninety years of leisure
Small precious things to guard,
  None else had time to treasure.

Their crystal was their pride,
  Their porcelain a token,
Kept safe until they died
  And handed on unbroken.

Colin Ellis

THE POOL

BETWEEN the cliff and the sea,
   On a blunt promontory bracken-fronted,
Where no tree is, only a twisted stunted
   Thorn, blown to one knee,

   Here you, small secret stream,
Come to fulfilment, spread your constant pool
To hold the radiant summer skies and cool
   Moonlight and star-gleam.

   How many torrents run
With chattering haste and clamour to the sea,
Lost in that vastness without memory
   Of any star or sun!

But you, through each long year,
Watch the thorn's Easter whiteness, and the red
Red berries for a crown about its head,
   The new leaf and the sere,

   Green bracken shoulder-high,
Bronzing and withered, through whose tangled
      ways
The rabbits bring their little ones and gaze
   Upon your mirrored sky.

   The seabirds flashing over,
Circling and crying till the bare cliff rings,
Reveal the hidden splendour of their wings
   To you as to a lover;

   And when the children chase
Their pleasure through the summer hours, you hear
Their voice, their laughter; see perchance sun-clear
   One maiden musing face.

                    P. Hugh B. Lyon

A LITTLE SOUND

A LITTLE sound—
  Only a little, a little—
The breath in a reed,
  A trembling fiddle;
The trumpet's ring,
  The shuddering drum;
So all the glory, bravery, hush
  Of music come.

A little sound—
  Only a stir and a sigh
Of each green leaf
  Its fluttering neighbour by;
Oak on to oak,
  The wide, dark forest through—
So o'er the watery wheeling world
  The night-winds go.

A little sound—
  Only a little, a little,
The thin, high drone
  Of the simmering kettle,
The gathering frost,
  The click of needle and thread,
Mother, the fading wall, the dream,
  The drowsy bed.

Walter de la Mare

BEAUTY'S FOR SHARING

AUNT MARY grows roses
  Old-fashioned and scented,
Tall hollyhocks which seem to reach up for the sky;
Wallflowers, sweet-william,
Great red-coated poppies
And velvety pansies all wide-eyed and shy.

Fine perfumed carnations,
Clematis, delphiniums
And love-in-a-mist form a gay tapestry
With humble dark monkshood,
White creeping convolvulus,
Maids' mutches, bachelors' buttons
And mauve honesty.

Seeds grow at a touch
From Aunt Mary's green fingers,
Pink ramblers cascade o'er her quaint rustic
    bowers:
And—" Come! They're for sharing,"
She'll say as she picks you
A basket brimful of her favourite flowers.

Mary M. Milne

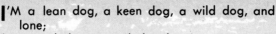

LONE DOG

I'M a lean dog, a keen dog, a wild dog, and
    lone;
I'm a rough dog, a tough dog, hunting on my own;
I'm a bad dog, a mad dog, teasing silly sheep;
I love to sit and bay the moon, to keep fat souls
    from sleep.

I'll never be a lap dog, licking dirty feet,
A sleek dog, a meek dog, cringing for my meat,
Not for me the fireside, the well-filled plate,
But shut door, and sharp stone, and cuff, and kick,
    and hate.

Not for me the other dogs, running by my side,
Some have run a short while, but none of them
    would bide.
O mine is still the lone trail, the hard trail, the
    best,
Wide wind, and wild stars, and the hunger of the
    quest!

Irene R. McLeod

I SAW A SHIP ...

I SAW a ship a-sailing, a-sailing, a-sailing,
    With emeralds and rubies and sapphires in her
       hold;
And a bosun in a blue coat bawling at the railing,
Piping through a silver call that had a chain of
       gold;
The summer wind was failing and the tall ship
       rolled.

I saw a ship a-steering, a-steering, a-steering,
With roses in red thread worked upon her sails;
With sacks of purple amethysts, the spoils of
       buccaneering,
Skins of musky yellow wine, and silks in bales,
Her merry men were cheering, hauling on the
       brails.

I saw a ship a-sinking, a-sinking, a-sinking,
With glittering sea-water splashing on her decks,
With seamen in her spirit-room singing songs and
       drinking,
Pulling claret bottles down, and knocking off the
       necks,
The broken glass was chinking as she sank among
       the wrecks.

John Masefield

SONG

THE lark now leaves his watery nest
   And climbing shakes his dewy wings;
He takes this window for the east,
   And to implore your light he sings.
Awake, awake! The morn will never rise
Till she can dress her beauty at your eyes.

The merchant bows unto the seaman's star,
   The ploughman from the sun his season takes;
And still the lover wonders what they are
   Who look for day before his mistress wakes.
Awake, awake! Break through your veils of lawn;
Then draw the curtains, and begin the dawn.

Sir William Davenant

DARBY AND JOAN

WHEN I'm an old lady
    And you're an old gent,
Shaky and quaky,
    Rheumatic and bent,

We'll walk in the harvest
    And see the gold leaf
(Enough of the heyday
    Of youth and its grief!).

What fun we will have
    When we're old and we're grey,
Chuckling and smiling
    The Winter away,

For Summer will come
    To a gouty old pair
With no-one to boss them
    And free as the air.

You'll lean on your stick
    And I'll carry my gamp,
And muggers will tremble
    To hear our feet tramp . . .

I'll come to your garden
    And smell the sweet scent,
When I'm an old lady
    And you're an old gent.

Elizabeth Borland

THE JOYS OF THE ROAD

NOW the joys of the road are chiefly these:
   A crimson touch on the hard-wood trees:
A vagrant's morning wide and blue,
In early fall, when the wind walks, too;
A shadowy highway, cool and brown,
Alluring up and enticing down
From rippled water to dappled swamp,
From purple glory to scarlet pomp;
The outward eye, the quiet will,
And the striding heart from hill to hill;
The tempter apple over the fence;
The cobweb bloom on the yellow quince;
The palish asters along the wood—
A lyric touch of the solitude;
An open hand, an easy shoe,
And a hope to make the day go through—
And O the joy that is never won,
But follows and follows the journeying sun,
By marsh and tide, by meadow and stream,
A will-o'-the wind, a light-o'-dream,
The racy smell of the forest loam,
When the stealthy, sad-heart leaves go home;
The broad gold wake of the afternoon;
The silent fleck of the cold new moon;
The sound of the hollow sea's release
From the stormy tumult to starry peace;
With only another league to wend;
And two brown arms at the journey's end!
These are the joys of the open road—
For him who travels without a load.

                      W. Bliss Carman

A ROOMFUL OF LEAVES

WHENEVER sunlight falls
        In a certain way,
The garden trees,
Shaken by summer breeze,
Invade my quiet room.
They bow and sway
Around me as I sit,
And the shadow play
Of leaves of beech and birch
And pear and lime,
Bring new magic
To the summer-time;
A roomful of leaves,
Exquisite, fragile, grey
Ghosts of the green ones;
Lovely leaves to stay
In memory and haunt
My little room still
On many a winter's day!

                Aileen E. Passmore

I'VE BEEN ROAMING

I'VE been roaming, I've been roaming,
  Where the meadow-dew is sweet,
And like a queen I'm coming
  With its pearls upon my feet.

I've been roaming, I've been roaming,
  O'er red rose and lily fair,
And like a sylph I'm coming
  With its blossoms in my hair.

I've been roaming, I've been roaming,
  Where the honeysuckle creeps,
And like a bee I'm coming
  With its kisses on my lips.

I've been roaming, I've been roaming,
  Over hill and over plain,
And like a bird I'm coming
  To my bower back again.

George Darley

THE WOOING OF KATY MORE

As I passed her cottage door,
   There sat little Katy More;
Round her neck and shoulders fair
Rippling hung her golden hair.

At my step she raised her head,
And her blue eyes, laughing, said,
" Did you, young man, ever see
A fresher little maid than me?"

And I answered, straight and plain,
" No, nor ever shall again;
Never mouth so sweet as this,"
Stealing, as I spoke, a kiss.

Then she turned with look askance,
Half bashful and half proud the glance,
When I, between her and the door,
Stepped, and kept my Katy More.

So I soothed her wounded pride,
Stood with her blushing side by side.
Half within, half out, that door,
I won my little Katy More.

Thomas Faed

INS AND OUTS

WHEN you wake up in the morning on the day
    of ' the great match ',
  And rush to the venetians for a peep,
And the rain-flouts flog the windows, and
    belabour the soaked thatch,
  And the world of leaves with water is a-weep;
When you think of sodden wickets, and of sawdust
    heaps, and steam,
  And instead of donning flannels with a shout,
You want to use strong language, and get back to
    bed, and dream—
  Oh! that is when a cricketer feels ' Out '!

But when the sloping sunbeams on the verdant turf
    shine warm
  And you tread the springing creases with a
    spring;
And the captain's won the toss, and you feel in
    rippin' form
  And you're sent in first to ' slog like anything ';
And you find the turf like velvet, and the first ball
    goes for six,
  And you've early premonitions of a win,
And you seem at peace with nature, and at home
    before the sticks—
  Oh! that is when a cricketer feels ' In '!

E. J. Milliken

THE PLOUGHMAN

WHERE upland winds are blowing
And skies are paly blue,
And hedges all have hills to climb
And level fields are few,

I love to watch the ploughman
Go slowly up the brae,
And reach the crest, a silhouette
Between me and the day.

And while the hedge beside me
Makes music in the wind,
I trace him where he moves unseen
By lapwing flights behind.

And from the newest furrow,
All glossy from the steel,
There glows a warmth within my heart
My fingers cannot feel.

But while I watch the ploughman,
All unresponsive he
Goes stolid, stolid, up and down,
And never looks at me.

Walter Wingate

COLOUR of lilac
    And laburnum gold,
Candles of chestnut
Lighted by the Spring,
Greenfinches unseen,
Lulling the tranquil hours,
Sheep voices from the fold
And swallows on the wing.

Bespangled meadows
And green willows blithe,
Small orchards blossom-clad,
The hedgerows white with may;
Old men a-talking
As the long grass falls
Before the swishing scythe,
And white-frocked girls at play.

Cuckoos calling
In the woods at morn,
Wallflowers basking
Round the sunken pool,
Windows opening
To far hillsides
Green with growing corn;
Smooth lawns all shadow-cool.

Reed-fringed river
Where the iris grows
And cows contented stand
In heat of day;
Long silent lanes
Whose cloistered hedges
Borrow the first wild rose
From June, for May.

D. Lovatt Williams

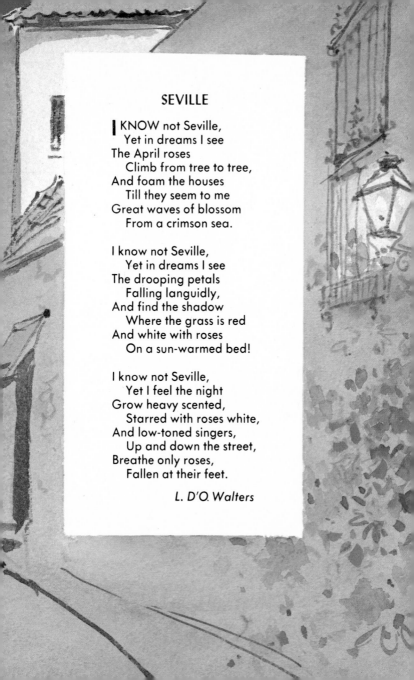

SEVILLE

I KNOW not Seville,
   Yet in dreams I see
The April roses
   Climb from tree to tree,
And foam the houses
   Till they seem to me
Great waves of blossom
   From a crimson sea.

I know not Seville,
   Yet in dreams I see
The drooping petals
   Falling languidly,
And find the shadow
   Where the grass is red
And white with roses
   On a sun-warmed bed!

I know not Seville,
   Yet I feel the night
Grow heavy scented,
   Starred with roses white,
And low-toned singers,
   Up and down the street,
Breathe only roses,
   Fallen at their feet.

L. D'O. Walters

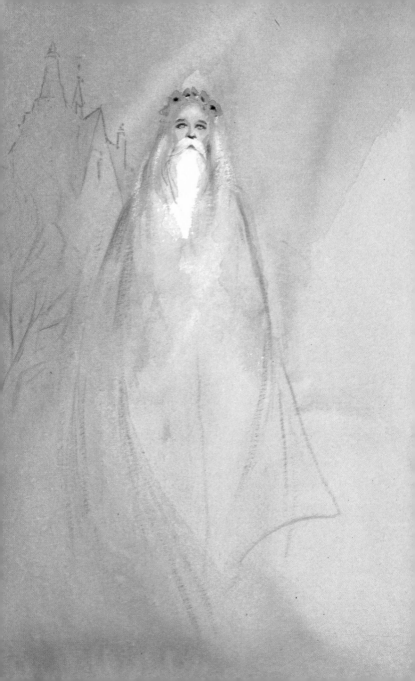

THE PRINCE OF SLEEP

I MET at eve the Prince of Sleep,
　　His was a still and lovely face;
He wandered through a valley steep,
　　Lovely in a lonely place.

His garb was grey of lavender,
　　About his brow a poppy-wreath
Burned like dim coals, and everywhere
　　The air was sweeter for his breath.

His twilight feet no sandals wore,
　　His eyes shone faint in their own flame,
Fair moths that gloomed his steps before
　　Seemed letters of his lovely name.

His house is in the mountain ways,
　　A phantom house of misty walls,
Whose golden flocks at evening graze,
　　And witch the moon with muffled calls.

Dark in his pools clear visions lurk,
　　And rosy, as with morning buds,
Along his dales of broom and birk
　　Dreams haunt his solitary woods.

I met at eve the Prince of Sleep,
　　His was a still and lovely face;
He wandered through a valley steep,
　　Lovely in a lonely place.

Walter de la Mare

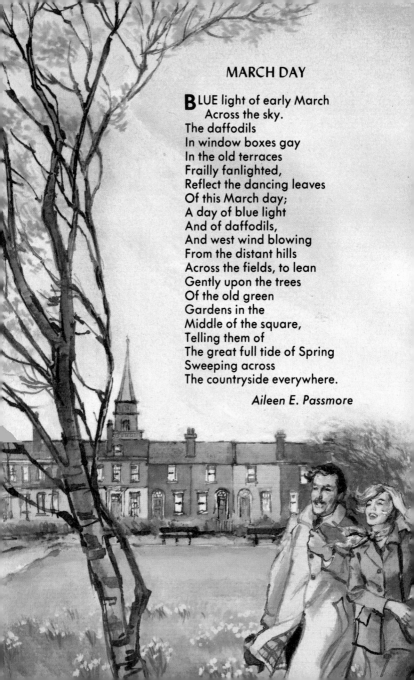

MARCH DAY

BLUE light of early March
 Across the sky.
The daffodils
In window boxes gay
In the old terraces
Frailly fanlighted,
Reflect the dancing leaves
Of this March day;
A day of blue light
And of daffodils,
And west wind blowing
From the distant hills
Across the fields, to lean
Gently upon the trees
Of the old green
Gardens in the
Middle of the square,
Telling them of
The great full tide of Spring
Sweeping across
The countryside everywhere.

Aileen E. Passmore

FOREFATHERS

HERE they went with smock and crook,
     Toiled in the sun, lolled in the shade,
Here they mudded out the brook
     And here their hatchet cleared the glade:
Harvest-supper woke their wit,
Huntsman's moon their wooings lit.

From this church they led their brides,
     From this church themselves were led
Shoulder-high; on these waysides
     Sat to take their beer and bread.
Names are gone—what men they were
These their cottages declare.

Names are vanished, save the few
     In the old brown Bible scrawled;
These were men of pith and thew,
     Whom the city never called;
Scarce could read or hold a quill,
Built the barn, the forge, the mill.

Unrecorded, unrenowned,
　　Men from whom my ways begin,
Here I know you by your ground
　　But I know you not within—
There is silence, there survives
Not a moment of your lives.

Like the bee that now is blown
　　Honey-heavy on my hand,
From his toppling tansy-throne
　　In the green tempestuous land—
I'm in clover now, nor know
Who made honey long ago.

Edmund Blunden

HOW DO I LOVE THEE?

HOW do I love thee? Let me count the ways.
  I love thee to the depth and breadth and
  height
My soul can reach, when feeling out of sight
For the ends of Being and ideal Grace.
I love thee to the level of every day's
Most quiet need, by sun and candle-light.
I love thee freely, as men strive for right;
I love thee purely, as they turn from praise.
I love thee with the passion put to use
In my old griefs, and with my childhood's faith.
I love thee with a love I seemed to lose
With my lost saints—I love thee with the breath,
Smiles, tears, of all my life!—and, if God choose,
I shall but love thee better after death.

Elizabeth Barrett Browning

CHLOE AND MYRA

CHLOE is elegant and pretty,
  But silly and affected;
Myra is sensible and witty,
  And by the wise respected.

When pretty Chloe I behold,
  I think myself her lover;
But ere I have my passion told,
  Her failings I discover.

When Myra talks, I'm pleased to hear,
  And venerate her mind;
But in her face no charms appear,
  My wavering heart to bind.

Blindfold I should to Myra run,
  And swear to love her ever;
Yet when the bandage was undone,
  Should only think her clever.

With the full usage of my eyes,
  I Chloe should decide for;
But when she talks, I *her* despise,
  Whom, dumb, I could have died for!

My ear or eye must tortur'd be
  If I make choice of either;
'Tis therefore best I should agree—
  Ladies!—to marry neither!

Lady Burrell

ROSES

A SEA of broom was on the brae;
   A heaven of speedwell lit the way;
But ever as I passed along
Of roses only was my song—
          Roses, roses, roses!

They spread their petals pink and white
Full stretch to feast upon the light;
They pushed each other on the spray
Like children mad with holiday—
          Roses, roses, roses!

But as when summer's noon is high
A tearful cloud bedims the sky,
A sudden memory of pain
Arises from the bright refrain—
          Roses, roses, roses!

I watch a figure to and fro
'Mong summer roses long ago—
Herself a rose as blithe as they.
Alas! How soon they pass away—
          Roses, roses, roses!

Walter Wingate

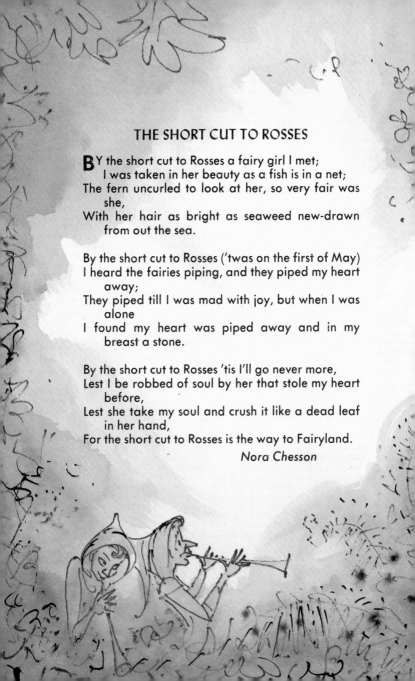

THE SHORT CUT TO ROSSES

BY the short cut to Rosses a fairy girl I met;
    I was taken in her beauty as a fish is in a net;
The fern uncurled to look at her, so very fair was
    she,
With her hair as bright as seaweed new-drawn
    from out the sea.

By the short cut to Rosses ('twas on the first of May)
I heard the fairies piping, and they piped my heart
    away;
They piped till I was mad with joy, but when I was
    alone
I found my heart was piped away and in my
    breast a stone.

By the short cut to Rosses 'tis I'll go never more,
Lest I be robbed of soul by her that stole my heart
    before,
Lest she take my soul and crush it like a dead leaf
    in her hand,
For the short cut to Rosses is the way to Fairyland.

Nora Chesson

ROBIN REDBREAST

GOOD-BYE, good-bye to Summer!
　　For Summer's nearly done;
The garden smiling faintly,
　　Cool breezes in the sun;
Our thrushes now are silent,
　　Our swallows flown away—
But Robin's here in coat of brown,
　　With ruddy breast-knot gay.
　　Robin, Robin Redbreast,
　　O Robin dear!
　　Robin singing sweetly
　　　　In the falling year.

Bright yellow, red, and orange,
　　The leaves come down in hosts;
The trees are Indian princes,
　　But soon they'll turn to ghosts;
The scanty pears and apples
　　Hang russet on the bough;
It's Autumn, Autumn, Autumn late
　　'Twill soon be Winter now.
　　Robin, Robin Redbreast,
　　O Robin dear!
　　And welladay! my Robin,
　　　　For pinching times are near.

The fireside for the cricket,
　　The wheatstack for the mouse,
When trembling night-winds whistle
　　And moan all round the house;
The frosty ways like iron,
　　The branches plumed with snow,—
Alas! in Winter, dead and dark,
　　Where can poor Robin go?
　　Robin, Robin Redbreast,
　　O Robin, dear!
　　And a crumb of bread for Robin,
　　　　His little heart to cheer.

William Allingham

THE WIND THAT SHAKES THE BARLEY

THERE'S music in my heart all day,
    I hear it late and early,
It comes from fields far, far away,
    The wind that shakes the barley.

Above the uplands drenched with dew,
    The sky hangs soft and pearly,
An emerald world is listening to
    The wind that shakes the barley.

Above the bluest mountain crest
    The lark is singing rarely,
It rocks the singer into rest,
    The wind that shakes the barley.

Oh, still through summers and through springs
    It calls me late and early,
Come home, come home, come home, it sings,
    The wind that shakes the barley.

Katharine Tynan

HEART OF GOLD

HARD-VISAGED winter
   In his iron hand
Holds all the land
Imprisoned
On this night
Of dark December;
Gone the spring's delight,
The glory of the summer,
Autumn mist—
Nothing can resist
This tyrant who has come—
But, here at home,
With firelight bright,
And lamp's warm light,
Away from dark and cold,
Why, winter here reveals
His heart of gold!

Aileen E. Passmore

NOCTURNE

A SENSE of stolen joy is mine
    To leave the village sleeping,
And with the music of my feet
To wake the echoes down the street,
    Where ne'er a light is peeping.

'Tis fine to hear the steeple clocks
    With weary voice and hollow
Discharge their conscientious twelves
As if they knew within themselves
    Of easier hours to follow.

Beneath the dim poetic moon
    The houses seem enchanted;
Their unromantic yesterday
Is charmed a thousand years away,
    And each is beauty-haunted.

And even the thoughts that come to me
    The strangest shapes are taking,
And smack of dream and shadow too
As if the night would claim her due
    From slumber or from waking!

Walter Wingate

GARDENS

I WANT to have a garden
  In a place beside the sea
Where stocks and phlox and hollyhocks
  Will nod their heads to me,
And where the morning sunshine
  Will make the garden bright
And the grey and misty waters
  Will sing to me at night.

I want to have a garden
  Where my friends can walk with me,
A friendly place, a quiet place
  Where peace comes dropping free
And laughter echoes down the paths
  And makes the garden gay,
While blue and sparkling waters
  Will sing to me all day.

I want to have a garden
  And it must be Ayrshire way,
Where green and friendly Carrick Hills
  Sweep upward from the bay,
And I shall live beside my flowers
  Under my rowan tree,
And the rolling Ayrshire waters
  Shall ever sing to me.

Dorothy Dunbar

BUCCANEER BILL

IF I were but a buccaneer,
  The seven seas I'd roam,
The wide green ocean for my road,
  A sailing ship my home.

The wind-swept deck beneath my feet,
  White sails above my head,
And the gentle, ever-rolling sea
  To rock me in my bed.

The whole wide world before me,
  My home left far behind,
The sights and sounds of foreign shores
  Forever in my mind.

I'd ply the ancient sailing routes
  The clippers took of old,
And sail around the Spanish Main
  In search of Spanish gold.

And when my wandering days be done,
  My roving days be through,
What splendid dashing tales I'd tell,
  About my gallant crew!

Oh, if I were but a buccaneer,
  The seven seas I'd roam,
To meet with great adventures,
  Far across the tossing foam.

Glenda Moore

THE MATCH

SHE had eyes of cornflower blue,
  While he had eyes of brown,
She loved the fresh pastoral view,
  Alas! he loved the town.

She liked to picnic on the green,
  Or on a tranquil shore,
While he preferred a livelier scene
  And loved the ocean's roar.

He liked to socialise each week,
  She didn't care to dance.
He, quick-tempered, she so meek,
  And yet this strange romance

Has lasted now for thirty years,
  They hope for sixty-four!
For they agreed to disagree
  And love—can I say more?

Elizabeth Borland

MARY

REBECCA has a special friend whom none of us
can see,
She always gets invited when Rebecca comes to tea;
She doesn't like to wash her hands and never eats
her bread,
And always wants to start to talk while grace is
being said.

When the meal is over she's the first one out to
play,
She hurries from the table without asking if she
may;
She likes to play at hide and seek, but cannot
count to ten,
She very quickly finds us and the game begins
again.

She shares Rebecca's bedroom as a very favoured
    guest,
She doesn't see the need for sleep, and hates to have
    to rest;
She always wants a story when it's time to go to
    bed,
And Rebecca has to stay up, too, until the book is
    read.

She wakes up very early, but she doesn't make a
    noise
Until she gets Rebecca up to play with all the toys.
Rebecca and her special friend—a really daunting
    pair—
One you see and one you don't, together
    everywhere!

Marion Elliott

TARANTELLA

DO you remember an Inn,
     Miranda?
Do you remember an Inn?
And the tedding and the spreading
Of the straw for a bedding,
And the fleas that tease in the High Pyrenees,
And the wine that tasted of the tar?
And the cheers and the jeers of the young
     muleteers
(Under the vine of the dark verandah)?
Do you remember an Inn, Miranda,
Do you remember an Inn?
And the cheers and the jeers of the young
     muleteers
Who hadn't got a penny,
And who weren't paying any,
And the hammer at the doors and the Din?
And the Hip! Hop! Hap!
Of the clap
Of the hands to the twirl and the swirl
Of the girl gone chancing,
Glancing,
Dancing,
Backing and advancing.
Snapping of the clapper to the spin
Out and in—
And the Ting, Tong, Tang of the Guitar!
Do you remember an Inn,
Miranda?
Do you remember an Inn?

                              Hilaire Belloc

SONNET

TO one who has been long in city pent,
 'Tis very sweet to look into the fair
And open face of heaven—to breathe a prayer
Full in the smile of the blue firmament.
Who is more happy, when, with heart's content,
Fatigued he sinks into some pleasant lair
Of wavy grass, and reads a debonair
And gentle tale of love and languishment?
Returning home at evening, with an ear
Catching the notes of Philomel—an eye
Watching the sailing cloudlet's bright career,
He mourns that day so soon has glided by,
E'en like the passage of an angel's tear
That falls through the clear ether silently.

John Keats

TOAST TO THE LADIES

HERE'S to the maiden of bashful fifteen;
　　Here's to the widow of fifty;
Here's to the flaunting extravagant quean,
　　And here's to the housewife that's thrifty.

Here's to the charmer whose dimples we prize;
　　Now to the maid who has none, sir;
Here's to the girl with a pair of blue eyes,
　　And here's to the nymph with but one, sir.

Here's to the maid with a bosom of snow;
　　Now to her that's as brown as a berry;
Here's to the wife with a face full of woe,
　　And now to the damsel that's merry.

For let 'em be clumsy, or let 'em be slim,
　　Young or ancient, I care not a feather;
So fill a pint bumper quite up to the brim,
So fill up your glasses, nay, fill to the brim,
　　And let us e'en toast them together.

Richard Brinsley Sheridan

THE PARSON'S POOL

WOULD you wish to know
    Where your angle to throw?
Try the Parson's Pool, the Parson's Pool;
    For the Parson, I'm told,
    Like the monks of old,
Ne'er wants a goodly fish in his Pool.

    The Pool is deep,
    And the Salmon leap,
In the moving cool, the moving cool;
    If you're anything sly,
    There cast your fly,
You're sure of a fish in the Parson's Pool.

    As I took my way,
    In the dawning grey,
By the Parson's Pool, the Parson's Pool;
    " You've no permission,"
    Cried a lad, " there to fish in;
Don't fish, if you please, in the Parson's Pool."

    But the moment he turned
    The advice I spurned,
Of the Parson's fool, the Parson's fool;
    And when no one was nigh,
    I dropt my fly,
And caught a fine fish in the Parson's Pool.

John Dunn

HOMESICK

I SHUT my eyes to rest 'em, just a bit ago it seems,
An' back among the Cotswolds I were wanderin' in me dreams.
I saw the old grey homestead, with the rickyard set around,
An' catched the lowin' of the herd, a pleasant, homelike sound.
Then on I went a-singin', through the pastures where the sheep
Was lyin' underneath the elms, a-tryin' for to sleep.

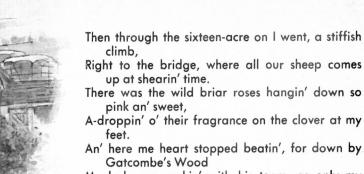

Then through the sixteen-acre on I went, a stiffish
  climb,
Right to the bridge, where all our sheep comes
  up at shearin' time.
There was the wild briar roses hangin' down so
  pink an' sweet,
A-droppin' o' their fragrance on the clover at my
  feet.
An' here me heart stopped beatin', for down by
  Gatcombe's Wood
My lad was workin' with his team, as only my
  lad could!

" *Come back!*" was what the tricklin' brook an'
  breezes seemed to say;
" *'Tis lonesome on the Cotswolds now that Mary
  Drew's away.*"
An' back again I'm goin' (for me wages has been
  paid,
An' they're lookin' through the papers for another
  kitchen maid).
Back to the old grey homestead, an' the uplands
  cool an' green,
To my lad among the Cotswolds, where me heart
  has always been!

Fay Inchfawn

A LATE SUMMER

SUMMER came today
  With sun and breeze;
Though the blossom trees
Are withered, yet
Summer flowers are
Growing in the sunshine:
The tall towers
Of blue delphiniums,
And the hollyhocks;
At their base the sweet
Night-scented stocks,
The roses opening out
To greet this day
Of first real warmth;
And all the bright array
Of alyssum and catmint,
And aubrietia blue.
Yes, summer came today,
It's really true
After so much rain
And wind,
Summer came today,
Out of the blue—
Long overdue!

Aileen E. Passmore

THE CORNFIELD

A CORNFIELD beside a lane,
   A lane beside a cornfield.
I know not how to put it plain,
So that no truth remain concealed,
No tithe of beauty unrevealed.

The lane has hawthorn hedgerows, knit
With bittersweet and parsley lace;
There hooded yellow-hammers sit,
And loose their notes of arrowy grace—
Arrows of gold time ne'er could face.

Beside an elm is set a gate,
A pleasant gate whereon to lean;
There one may lounge, there one may wait,
And through the knapweed's crimson screen,
Watch yellow come upon the green

Of standing corn, all hushed and still,
In secret ranks of import strange—
An army with an unknown will,
O'er which swift scouting swallows range,
Yet bring no news of word or change.

The hedge the gate the birds the corn
The blossom and the bowering tree—
Give these, and give a harvest morn
Bending in beauty over me,
I ask no more. What more could be?

John S. Martin

A COUNTRY HOLIDAY

NOW in the waning ot summer these stony moorlands
    Are purple and gold with gorse and mingled heath,
The brambles down by the beck are black with berries,
    Fostered by suns overhead and the waters beneath.

The path we tread is a sheep-track buried in heather,
    Or an old Celt road with cart-ruts scoring the way,
Till the steep last rise is passed, and shining below us
    The harbour thrusts like a scimitar into the bay.

Happy it is to go back to a place remembered,
    To watch it change and unfold as the road winds down;
Each name on lintel and wall is a voice to call us
    Through alley and tumbling lane to the heart of the town.

There's wind in the harbour and white-tipped waves, masts rocking,
    A high tide running atilt at the gray sea wall,
A dancing boat with the sun in her sails bound outward,
    And the white gulls flying and crying over all.

This simple country, stern, beloved Cornwall,
    Purged by the winds, clean-mated with the sea,
This coloured corner of England—O earth-caged spirit,
    This is your heaven,—spread wings, come forth, come free!

P. Hugh B. Lyon

THE WILD GEESE

SOMETHING told the wild geese
   It was time to go.
Though the field lay golden
   Something whispered, ' Snow.'

Leaves were green and stirring,
   Berries, lustre-glossed,
But beneath warm feathers
   Something cautioned, ' Frost.'

All the sagging orchards
   Steamed with amber spice,
But each wild breast stiffened
   At remembered ice.

Something told the wild geese
   It was time to fly—
Summer sun was on their wings,
   Winter in their cry.

Rachel Field

GO DOWN TO KEW

GO down to Kew in lilac-time, in lilac-time, in
    lilac-time;
Go down to Kew in lilac-time (it isn't far from
    London!)
And you shall wander hand in hand with love in
    Summer's wonderland;
Go down to Kew in lilac-time (it isn't far from
    London!)

The cherry trees are seas of bloom and soft
    perfume and sweet perfume,
The cherry trees are seas of bloom (and oh! so
    near to London!)
And there they say, when dawn is high, and all the
    world's a blaze of sky,
The cuckoo, though he's very shy, will sing a song
    for London.

For Noah hardly knew of a bird of any kind that
    isn't heard
At Kew, at Kew, in lilac-time (and oh! so near to
    London!)
And when the rose begins to pout, and all the
    chestnut spires are out,
You'll hear the rest without a doubt, all chorusing
    for London:-

Come down to Kew in lilac-time, in lilac-time, in
    lilac-time,
Come down to Kew in lilac-time (it isn't far from
    London!)
And you shall wander hand in hand with love in
    Summer's wonderland;
Come down to Kew in lilac-time (it isn't far from
    London!)

Alfred Noyes

MY EARLY HOME

HERE sparrows build upon the trees,
    And stockdove hides her nest;
The leaves are winnowed by the breeze
    Into a calmer rest:
The black-cap's song was very sweet,
    That used the rose to kiss;
It made the Paradise complete;
    My early home was this.

The red-breast from the sweetbrier bush
    Dropt down to pick the worm;
On the horse-chestnut sang the thrush,
    O'er the house where I was born;
The moonlight, like a shower of pearls,
    Fell o'er this ' bower of bliss ',
And on the bench sat boys and girls;
    My early home was this.

The old house stooped just like a cave,
    Thatched o'er with mosses green;
Winter around the walls would rave,
    But all was calm within;
The trees are here all green again,
    Here bees the flowers still kiss,
But flowers and trees seemed sweeter then:
    My early home was this.

J. Clare

MY LOVE

MY love is fair, she is better than fair to me:
    She puts me in mind of a wild white seagull
    flying over the sea;
She puts me in mind of a dim wind going softly in
    the grass—
Of things remembered, and young things, and
    things that shall come to pass.

Always from a boy, as I walked the evening
    road
And saw the curtained windows where the warm
    light glowed,
I have desired little children, and old songs, and
    sleep,
And an ache has come in my throat for the need I
    had to weep.

But now the doors of all kind homes have I passed
    through,
And found the room of my own heart warm and
    bright with you,
And found little children there, playing round the
    fire,
And found the peace that is dreamier than sleep,
    and the songs beyond desire.

Gerald Gould

FOUR AND EIGHT

THE foxglove by the cottage door
Looks down on Joe, and Joe is Four.

The foxglove by the garden gate
Looks down on Joan, and Joan is Eight.

" I'm glad we're small," said Joan, " I love
To see inside the fox's glove,
Where taller people cannot see,
And all is ready for the bee;
The door is wide, the feast is spread,
The walls are dotted rosy red;"
" And only little people know
How nice it looks in there," said Joe.
Said Joan, " The upper rooms are locked;
A bee went buzzing up——he knocked,
But no one let him in, so then
He bumbled gaily down again."
" Oh, dear!" sighed Joe, " if only we
Could grow as little as that bee,
We too might room by room explore
The foxglove by the cottage door."

The foxglove by the garden gate
Looked down and smiled on Four and Eight.

Ffrida Wolfe

THE SPRING

NOW that the winter's gone, the earth has lost
  Her snow-white robes; and now no more
  the frost
Candies the grass, or casts an icy cream
Upon the silver lake or crystal stream.

But the warm sun thaws the benumbed earth,
And makes it tender; gives a second birth
To the dead swallows; wakes in hollow trees
The drowsy cuckoo and the humble bees.

Now do a choir of chirping minstrels bring
In triumph to the world the youthful spring:
The valleys, hills, and woods in rich array,
Welcome the coming of the longed-for May.

Thomas Carew

ACKNOWLEDGMENTS

Our thanks to the Society of Authors and Miss Pamela Hinkson for *The Cuckoo* and *The Wind that Shakes the Barley* by Katharine Tynan Hinkson; to the Society of Authors and the Literary Trustees of Walter de la Mare for *A Little Sound* and *The Prince of Sleep;* to the Society of Authors as the Literary Representatives of the Estate of John Masefield for *I Saw a Ship;* to Ward Lock Ltd. for *Homesick* by Fay Inchfawn; to Marion Elliott for *Time for Play* and *Mary;* to P. Hugh B. Lyon for *The Pool* and *A Country Holiday;* to Mary M. Milne for *Beauty's for Sharing;* to Elizabeth Borland for *Darby and Joan* and *The Match;* to Charles Griffiths for *A Roomful of Leaves, Heart of Gold* and *A Late Summer* by Aileen E. Passmore; to Mary McKerrow for *The Wooing of Kate More* by Thomas Faed; to Dorothy Dunbar for *Gardens;* to Glenda Moore for *Buccaneer Bill.*